Introduction

A garnish is the final touch to a dish, its purpose to decorate and to enhance the flavour, making the food a delight to behold as well as to eat. The senses are all important to the enjoyment of a meal, not only taste and aroma, but also sight. Flavour really does improve when food looks good too, so it's worth taking a little extra time over the presentation of a dish that has been carefully prepared. It will always be appreciated.

The simplest garnishes are often the best – a fresh herb sprig, a scattering of hot, toasted almond flakes, juicy wedges of lemon for squeezing. The only rules are that the garnish is fresh, and that it complements the taste of the food. Use the ingredients in the dish you are garnishing as inspiration.

When I began writing this book I perused cookware shops and department stores and found many strange-looking gadgets designed to help make garnishes – such bizarre contraptions, it was sometimes hard to ascertain their uses! Good garnishing does not mean buying dozens of pieces of equipment which will spend most of their lives in a kitchen drawer. There are some useful tools, shown overleaf, which make preparation simpler and give good professional results, but the chances are you will already have most of them.

For attractive, creative garnishes the best tools are the imagination and the bounty of colours, flavours and textures available in our supermarkets, greengrocers and storecupboards.

Here I've tried to provide an abundance of garnishing and decorating ideas – both sweet and savoury – some very simple and others a little more elaborate. The techniques are easy-to-follow, so master the art of garnishing. Turn your food into a visual feast.

Lyn Rutherford

Equipment

As I have already mentioned, you don't need a comprehensive batterie de cuisine to prepare the garnishes in this book, but there are a few essentials most of which will already be part of the cooking enthusiast's kitchen. A good smooth heat-resistant work surface is important, so too is a large chopping board. Sharp knives are, of course, a must, but you don't need to fork out on a vast expensive range. Two knives take me through most of the cutting and chopping I ever have to do. The first is a large cook's knife with a curving 20-25cm (8-10 inch) blade for chopping, slicing, dicing and cutting up larger pieces of food. The second is a sharp, pointed paring knife which, together with a good pair of kitchen scissors, takes care of everything else.

The following inexpensive tools are also useful:

- Vegetable peeler: for peeling and paring rinds.
- Apple corer: for coring and cutting out small discs.
- Canelle knife: for cutting even-sized grooves in fruit and vegetable skins and firm flesh.
- Zester: to remove long pith-free threads of zest quickly from citrus fruits.
- Melon baller: for melon, butter and potato balls, but also for coring and scooping out the flesh from halved fruit, and for mini-scoops of ices and sorbets.
- Plain, fluted and fancy cutters: for croûtons, pastry, fruit and vegetable shapes, chocolate etc.
- Hinged frying basket: effectively two small metal sieves hinged together. Used for frying potato baskets, pastry and poppadum baskets. You can use two metal ladles or sieves held one inside the other for a similar effect.
- Piping bag and nozzles: two fluted nozzles (1 large, 1 medium) and two plain nozzles (1 large, 1 small) are all you need for piping cream, potato, vegetable purées, soft cheese, chocolate, toppings and fillings. Two nylon piping bags (1 large, 1 medium) are useful, and you can make small greaseproof piping bags whenever you need them.

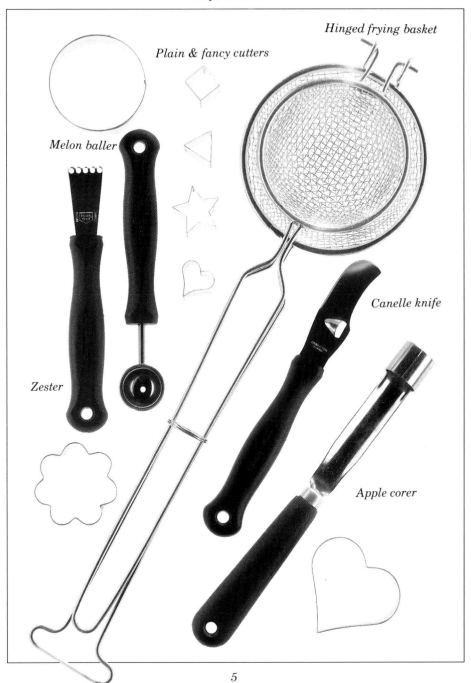

Hinged frying basket

Plain & fancy cutters

Melon baller

Canelle knife

Zester

Apple corer

Herbs

The simplest of garnishes are often the most effective. A fresh, aromatic flourish of greenery always enhances food whether it's a subtle scattering of snipped chives, a frosted geranium leaf, a perky tarragon sprig or a larger fragrant bouquet, chosen to complement the flavour of the dish.

Basil

Of the many varieties, sweet basil is the most common. Its rich, spicy smell and flavour, reminiscent of cloves, epitomizes the taste of the Mediterranean. Basil needs a good deal of sun to grow and is therefore mostly available from late spring throughout the summer, but it is well worth trying to nurture small plants on a kitchen shelf in winter.

The aromatic flavour marries wonderfully with tomatoes, mushrooms, lemon and garlic in Italian, Indian and Thai dishes. The large 'lettuce leaf' variety and the striking purple basil are especially good torn into pieces and tossed into salads. Otherwise to garnish use the leaves torn, chopped or shredded for sprinkling, or be generous with sprigs.

Borage

This small summer herb with bright blue, star-like flowers has a flavour not unlike that of cucumber. The leaves and flowers are used as a fragrant and decorative addition to summer drinks and infusions. Borage is also popular in Italian cooking. Try using it to flavour the mild, creamy native cheeses of mascarpone and ricotta. Enliven green salads with the brilliant blue flowers or use them fresh or candied to decorate cakes and desserts.

Chervil

Chervil, with its soft feathery leaves and delicate anise flavour, is popular in France. It goes well with chicken, vegetables, fish and eggs. The flavour is lost quickly after chopping, so tear or roughly chop only, and add by the handful to salads or sprinkle generously over soups. A single dainty sprig of chervil makes a graceful garnish.

Purple basil

Chervil

Sweet basil

Borage

Chives

Chives are the smallest member of the onion family with a grass-like appearance and a mild onion flavour. The fine hollow stems are chopped or snipped and used to flavour all manner of foods, including omelettes and other egg dishes, fish, cheeses, potatoes, creamy soups and salads.

Sprinkle snipped chives to garnish or use whole ones, long and straight, or tied in bows or knots. Chives make natural 'string' for tying elegant bundles of food and the pretty mauve flowers are an attractive garnish scattered on to salads, soups or hors d'oeuvres.

Chinese Garlic Chives

Garlic or Chinese chives (Kuchai) have larger flat leaves and white flowers, with a distinctly garlic flavour. Use in more robust salads and oriental dishes in the same way as chives.

Coriander

Often called Chinese parsley, this is similar in appearance to flat-leaf parsley but has a flavour all its own. To tell the difference first look closely – the leaves are more rounded and you are most likely to buy coriander bundled up roots and all, whereas parsley always comes trimmed. Next, crush a leaf or two between the fingers to release the characteristic sweet, scented aroma – sometimes described, by non-enthusiasts, as 'soapy' or even 'fetid'.

Coriander is available all year round. Buy it in large bunches from Asian or Greek foodstores or pre-packed in supermarkets. Keep a bunch in a jug or vase of water, as you would cut flowers. Coriander is essential in Indian, Thai and Mexican cooking and is also used in Chinese, Middle Eastern and Greek dishes. The flavour goes well with fish, lamb, tomatoes, onion and other vegetables. Use whole sprigs to garnish, or roughly chop or tear the leaves to sprinkle. The leaves wilt quickly, so add just before serving.

Garlic chives

Chives

Coriander

Dill

With its fragrant feathery leaves tasting sweetly of anise, dill has a particular affinity with fish – especially salmon, trout and shellfish. It is also known for its inclusion in pickled cucumbers and the Scandinavian salmon dish 'gravlax'. When cooked dill quickly loses its flavour, so add it at the last minute or use it to its best advantage in cold dishes. It is delicious in salads: cucumber is a classic partner; eggs, chicken, pasta, rice, sour cream, yogurt and soft cheeses are all enhanced by this distinctive herb.

Fennel

Sweet fennel has a strong aniseed flavour with a slightly bitter tang. It is available through summer and early autumn. The leaves of the vegetable Florence fennel can be used in the same way but they have a more delicate flavour. Use both the frond-like leaves and the clusters of mustard-yellow flowers as a garnish for fish and shellfish, pork and egg dishes, or snip into salads and dressings.

Lemon Balm

Lemon scented and mint-like in appearance, the yellow-green variegated variety is particularly pretty and fresh looking. Use in savoury dishes, such as stuffings for chicken, pork and lamb; it is also good with fresh mild cheese. Add lemon balm to fruit drinks and punches and use sprigs as a garnish wherever you might otherwise use mint.

Marigold

Available from June to the first frosts, the vibrant golden yellow petals of the marigold flower have long been used in cookery as a flavouring and a dye. Sprinkle petals over exotic rice dishes, on to soups and into leafy salads.

Dill

Lemon balm

Fennel

Marjoram & Oregano

Both herbs have a warm, sweet and spicy scent although oregano (or wild marjoram) is the strongest and spiciest of the two. The Italians use oregano with abandon in pasta sauces, stews, salads and, of course, on pizzas. The Greeks love it too.

Use oregano more sparingly than marjoram as it is a lot more robust, but chop both into stews and soups, sauces, salads and marinades for grilled meat and fish. Scatter small sprigs and leaves generously.

Mint

There are many varieties of mint – spearmint or garden mint – being the most common. Available from late spring throughout summer the clean, refreshing flavour is unmistakable. Peppermint is most commonly used for flavouring candies and in the liqueur creme-de-menthe. Eau-de-cologne mint has an orangey perfumed flavour and darker leaves.

Use mint with lamb, shellfish, chicken, rice and of course potatoes for summery freshness. With hot spicy food a minted accompaniment serves as cool relief.

Add chopped mint to salads and dressings, fruit salads and ices. Add sprigs to cooling summer drinks and use as a garnish for savoury and sweet dishes alike. Simple desserts can be transformed by fresh fruit garnishes embellished with mint.

Nasturtium

With brilliantly coloured orange and red trumpet-like flowers and pretty, pepper-flavoured leaves, nasturtiums provide a colourful, dainty garnish for sweet and savoury dishes. Buy them pre-packed from larger supermarket salad counters in the summer or grow them in the garden. As you would expect from a member of the cress family, the flavour goes well with egg dishes and seafood. Try using nasturtium leaves as a bed instead of lettuce. Toss both flowers and leaves into salads.

Dwarf marjoram

Oregano

Mint

Sweet marjoram

Parsley

The most widely known herb, parsley is usually easy to buy. The dense curly variety we are most familiar with seems to have lost favour to the flat-leaved Italian or Greek parsley when it's available. The flavour of this is stronger and its long slender stalks and pretty leaves make an elegant garnish. Either way parsley enhances most savoury dishes of meat, fish, poultry, cheese, eggs and vegetables, bringing out the flavour of other herbs and seasonings.

Chop fine or coarse for sprinkling, or use sprigs to garnish. Chewing on parsley sprigs freshens the breath and so a sprig or two as a garnish can be more than just decorative, particularly with garlicky, spicy or fishy foods.

Rosemary

A highly aromatic Mediterranean herb with needle-shaped green or greyish-green leaves, rosemary is available all year round. During the summer it is further enhanced by small, delicate blue flowers.

Rosemary is traditional with lamb but also has a great affinity to veal, pork, chicken, lemon and potatoes. I particularly love fish and seafood garnished with rosemary sprigs before grilling or barbecueing. The leaves are a bit spiky for sprinkling as a garnish unless well chopped, but a sprig or two on a casserole or hot dish won't wilt.

Sage

A powerful, pungent herb. Its soft, downy velvet leaves are most commonly grey-green, but there are also attractive variegated, golden and purple varieties. Usually used in stuffings for roast pork and poultry, sage is also delicious in creamy sauces with veal, liver, bacon and cheese. I love it with fresh lime or lemon as a marinade for chicken, pork or shellfish. Use chopped or shredded or as sprigs to garnish. Include whole leaves with sautés and meat or fish kebabs.

Flat-leaved parsley

Sage

Rosemary

Curly parsley

Scented Geranium

Lemon, orange, rose, apple and peppermint are just some of the varieties of the scented geranium. The fragrant leaves can be chopped and used to flavour cakes, fruit salads, ices and sorbets, jellies and soft creamy cheeses. Use leaves, frosted if you prefer, to decorate cakes and desserts, especially soft fruit ones.

Sweet Cicely

An old-fashioned herb with exceptionally pretty, feathery, fern-like leaves. In early summer months tiny white flowerheads add to its charm. Sweet cicely has a sugar-sweet mild aniseed scent and flavour. Chop into fruit salads, compotes, sorbets and ice cream to flavour and sweeten – or simply adorn desserts with the dainty stems – much more stylish than mint.

Tarragon

Long-stalked with branching silvery green leaves, French tarragon has a strongly pungent flavour which belies its rather elegant gently curving stems. The distinctive aniseed flavour is very popular, harmonising with all kinds of food. It is most often combined with chicken and fish but is also good in egg dishes, mayonnaise and creamy sauces, savoury butters and green salads. Strip the leaves from the stalks to add to salads and sauces, and sprinkle over dishes, or chop finely if you prefer. Sprigs look graceful but wilt quickly so add just before serving.

Thyme

There are several varieties of this familiar bushy herb with its tiny leaves and woody stems, including golden lemon thyme with its distinctive flavour. In the summer months, common garden thyme has pretty clusters of mauve-pink flowers.

Thyme is especially good in rich red meat dishes, but is also delicious with chicken and other birds in stuffings and marinades. Use it with Mediterranean vegetables, such as tomatoes, aubergines (eggplant), peppers and mushrooms.

Peppermint-scented geranium

Lemon-scented geranium

Variegated lemon-scented
geranium

Tarragon

Thyme

Sweet cicely

Vegetable Julienne

Fine vegetable julienne makes an elegant garnish. They are often called 'matchsticks' as this well describes the shape and size – approximately 6cm × 5mm × 5mm (2½ × ¼ × ¼ inch). It takes time to prepare these uniform shapes, but they are a stylish garnish which can be raw or crisply cooked. Choose one vegetable or create a colourful blend of different flavours, all evenly prepared. Use hot or cold to garnish savoury dishes, as a border for meat and fish platters or tie into pretty bundles (see page 20).

Suitable vegetables are carrots, courgettes (zucchini), celery, turnips, swede, peppers, fennel, parsnip, celeriac, large radish, cucumber, beetroot and potato.

Julienne

1 Peel the vegetables and trim off all rounded edges to give an even squared shape. Cut into lengths approximately 6cm (2½ inches) long.

2 Using a sharp cook's knife, cut the vegetable pieces lengthwise into equal 5mm (¼ inch) slices. Stack 3 or 4 slices on top of each other and cut into even sticks.

Pommes Allumettes

Pommes allumettes, or 'potato matchsticks' are a classic French garnish for meat and fish dishes, especially grills.

1 Cut potato into fine julienne, about 3mm (⅛ inch) thick, as described above. Soak in cold water for at least 20 minutes, then drain and dry thoroughly.

2 Deep fry in hot oil, in batches if necessary, for a few minutes until deep golden in colour. Drain on absorbent kitchen paper and serve immediately, sprinkled with salt.

Julienne of yellow, green and red pepper; celery julienne; pommes allumettes and carrot julienne

Vegetable Bundles

Lightly cooked vegetables divided into neat little bundles are a colourful garnish either on individual servings or celebration platters, such as Christmas turkey or a special Sunday roast.

To tie up the bundles, you can use chives as edible 'string' or thin strips of leek or cucumber peel. Alternatively, for extra colour, hold vegetables in thinly sliced onion or chilli rings or contrasting hoops of carrot or courgette (zucchini).

Suitable vegetables are fine green beans, asparagus, baby carrots, baby sweetcorn, vegetable bâtons (page 24) and julienne (page 18).

Whole Vegetable Bundles

1 Prepare vegetables: top and tail green beans; break off woody stems from asparagus; trim tops off corn cobs and carrots.

2 To make hoops of carrot to hold vegetable bundles, peel a large carrot and slice into rings. Use a corer to remove the centre of the slices. Prepare courgette (zucchini) hoops in the same way.

3 Cook the vegetables (separately if preparing more than one) in boiling water until just cooked but still quite firm. Drain thoroughly.

4 Arrange the vegetables like bundles of twigs in the prepared hoops, or use onion slices or edible 'string', such as chives to hold them. Add an extra tiny spray of herbs if you like.

Julienne Bundles

1 Use one vegetable or choose a colourful assortment and prepare julienne (see page 18). Blanch in boiling water for 1-2 minutes, then drain.

2 Use whole chives to tie up small bundles of julienne.

Baby corn bundles, julienne bundles, asparagus bundles, green bean bundles and carrot bundles

Ribbons, Curls & Spirals

A colourful medley of ribbon-like vegetable strands makes an attractive hot or cold garnish, especially arranged as an elegant border for a dinner party platter. Light, pretty curls and spirals also make a decorative border garnish, but work equally well arranged as clusters of colour on all kinds of savoury dishes.

Suitable vegetables for ribbons are carrots, courgettes (zucchini) and small or medium-sized leeks. For curls, use carrots, courgettes and cucumber. To make spirals, use vegetables which are straight in shape, such as carrots, courgettes, cucumber and small mooli radish.

Vegetable Ribbons
1 Using a potato peeler and, pressing fairly firmly, peel whole lengths of carrot and courgette (zucchini). Simply quarter leeks lengthwise to give long bands.
2 Blanch or stir-fry to give tender ribbons.

Vegetable Curls
1 Prepare carrots and courgettes (zucchini) as for ribbons (step 1). Make cucumber curls in the same way but use only the dark green skin. Roll up each vegetable ribbon and secure with a cocktail stick.
2 Leave to stand in a bowl of iced water for at least 1 hour. When required, drain and remove cocktail sticks.

Vegetable Spirals
1 Trim vegetables to 7.5-10cm (3-4 inch) lengths. Push a wooden skewer right through each one from end to end.
2 Using a small, sharp knife and starting 5mm (¼ inch) from one end, cut through to the wooden skewer, then holding the vegetable in one hand and the knife in the other continue cutting around the skewer, rotating the vegetable until the other end is reached. Remove skewer.

Courgette (zucchini) and carrot curls; courgette and cucumber spirals; courgette and carrot ribbons

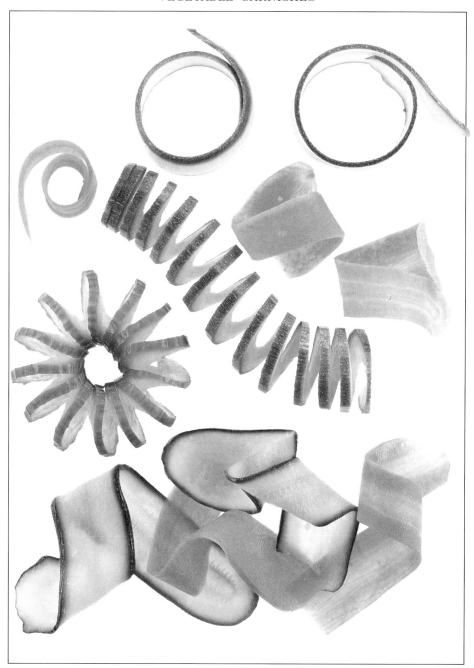

Bâtons & Chiselled Vegetables

Useful ways of trimming larger vegetables into smaller, more elegant shapes suitable for garnishing. Bâtons are even lengths. Chiselled vegetables are pared or turned in a chiselling fashion, similar to sharpening a pencil.

Suitable vegetables for bâtons are carrots, parsnips, courgettes (zucchini) and celery. For chiselled vegetables use courgettes, potatoes, swede and turnips.

Carrot & Parsnip Bâtons
Cut each vegetable in half across the middle, then cut the thinner part lengthwise in half and the thickest part into quarters. Long carrots or parsnips may need to be cut cross-wise into three or four pieces. The result is even pieces similar to baby vegetables in shape and size. Cook until just tender, drain and sprinkle with sesame seeds if you like.

Celery & Courgette (Zucchini) Bâtons
Cut the vegetables into 4 × 1cm (1½ × ½ inch) lengths. Blanch or use raw.

Chiselled Courgettes (Zucchini)
Cut the courgettes (zucchini) into 5cm (2 inch) lengths. Using a vegetable paring knife, chisel or sharpen both ends of each piece, discarding the trimmings.

Chiselled Potatoes, Swede & Turnips
Peel medium or large potatoes or small swede and cut into smaller elongated pieces. Using a vegetable paring knife trim or turn each piece to make rounded barrel shapes. Peel and cut into 2 or 3 thick slices across the middle. Trim or turn each piece to give 'baby vegetables'.

Parsnip bâtons, celery bâtons, chiselled turnips, chiselled courgettes (zucchini) and carrot bâtons

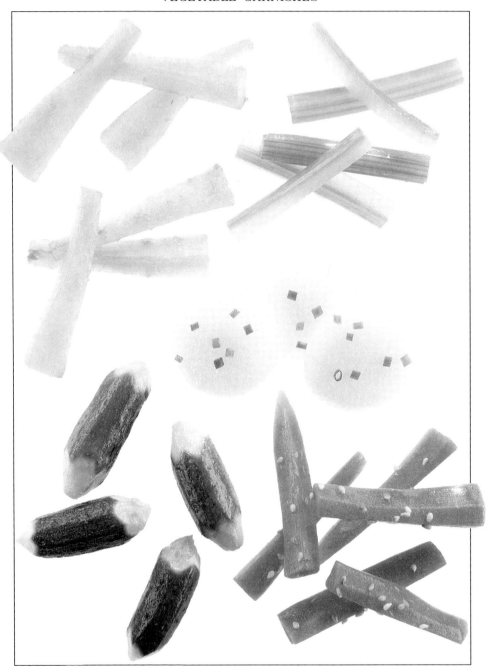

Vegetable Fans

Vegetable fans are one of the simplest garnishes to make. Use to garnish cold fish and meat platters, pâtés, salads, shellfish, etc. Delicate fleurs-de-lys are especially pretty as a garnish for oriental dishes.

Suitable vegetables are avocados, cucumber and gherkins.

Cucumber Fans

1 Cut a 2.5cm (1 inch) piece of cucumber on a slight diagonal. Use a canelle knife to remove strips of peel lengthwise if you wish. Cut in half lengthwise.

2 Lay each cucumber piece on its flat side. Using a sharp knife, and taking care not to cut right through to the opposite edge, cut into thin slices following the diagonal.

3 Gently flatten the cucumber slices to 'fan' out.

Cucumber Fleurs-de-Lys

Prepare as for cucumber fans (steps 1 & 2), then gently bend and tuck every other slice towards the joined end of the fan, leaving the alternate slices straight. Leave to stand in iced water for at least 1 hour before using.

Gherkin Fans

Using a small sharp knife and leaving one end intact, thinly slice the gherkin lengthwise. Flatten out to form a 'fan'. Add a chive or blanched pepper knot if you like.

Avocado Fans

Halve, stone and peel an avocado. Leaving the thin stem end intact, slice lengthwise. Gently flatten out to form a 'fan' and brush with lemon juice to prevent discolouring.

Cucumber Twists

Pile two or three thin slices of cucumber on top of each other and make a cut from the centre to the edge. Twist each side of the cut in opposite directions.

Gherkin fans, cucumber fleurs-de-lys, cucumber fan, avocado fan and cucumber twists

Vegetable Tassels

A quick, fun garnish for oriental dishes, savoury dips, cheese-boards, savoury tarts, flans and salads.

Suitable vegetables are spring onions (green shallots) and celery.

Spring Onion (Green Shallot) Tassels
1 Trim off the base and remove any untidy outer leaves. Trim off and discard the dark green parts, leaving a 7.5cm (3 inch) length.
2 With a sharp knife cut down the length of the spring onion (shallot), leaving about 2.5cm (1 inch) of the bulb end intact. Rotate the onion a quarter-turn and make another cut in the same way. Continue making as may cuts as possible to form thin tassel strands.
3 Leave to stand in iced water for at least 30 minutes until curled.

Double-ended Tassels
1 Prepare as for spring onion (green shallot) tassels (step 1).
2 Leaving about 2cm ($^{3}/_{4}$ inch) intact in the middle, feather both ends of the spring onion to form thin tassel strands.
3 Leave to stand in iced water for at least 30 minutes until curled.

Celery Tassels
Cut celery into 5cm (2 inch) lengths. Make lengthwise cuts down the celery, leaving about 2cm ($^{3}/_{4}$ inch) intact at the base, to make fine tassel strands. Leave to stand in iced water for at least 30 minutes until curled.

Spring onion (shallot) tassels; double-ended tassel, celery tassels

Vegetable Flowers

I am always intrigued when something is not quite what it seems. When served a dish with an exotic flower garnish it surprises me that anyone would take the trouble or have enough time to prepare such a creation. However I have discovered that these impressive, intriguing little blossoms are really quite simple to make. The colours and textures of the vegetables are delightful enough to compensate for imperfections. Make the flowers realistic by adding stalks and leaves using chives, herb sprigs and other greenery.

Suitable vegetables are chillis, radishes, tomatoes, turnips and courgettes (zucchini). Cut-out flowers of all kinds can be made from other vegetables, such as peppers, carrots, cucumber, aubergine (eggplant) and onions.

Radish Bud

1 Trim the stalk end of the radish to give a flat base. Using a vegetable paring knife make 5 or 6 vertical cuts almost to the base, then give the radish a quarter-turn and make 5 or 6 criss-cross cuts to give a grid pattern.
2 Gently push the 'petals' in a random fashion.
3 Add mint or other herb leaves or chive stalks.

Radish Flower

1 Proceed as for radish bud (step 1). Sprinkle liberally with salt and leave for at least 30 minutes to soften.
2 Rinse thoroughly, pat dry with absorbent kitchen paper and gently flatten the petals to form an open flower. For the centre add a small circle of pepper or carrot, or a tiny pile of caviar or lumpfish roe. Add greenery as above.

Chilli Flower

Use small to medium chillis. With a small sharp knife and leaving about 2.5cm (1 inch) intact at the stalk end, make lengthwise slits right through the tip. Discard the seeds. Leave to stand in iced water for at least 1 hour to curl.

Radish flowers, radish bud and chilli flowers

Turnip Chrysanthemum
1 Peel a small, round turnip and cut as for radish bud (step 1). Sprinkle liberally with salt and leave for at least 30 minutes to soften.
2 Rinse thoroughly and pat dry with absorbent kitchen paper. Push the 'petals' in a random fashion and add flat-leaved parsley sprigs, dill or other greenery.

Tomato Rose
1 Using a small sharp knife, thinly peel a firm tomato, starting at the bottom, to give one continuous spiral of skin.
2 Roll up the tomato skin to form a 'rose'. Secure with a piece of cocktail stick and open out the 'petals' slightly for a realistic look. Add basil leaves.

Cherry Tomato Flower
1 Place the cherry tomato stalk end down on a board. Using a small, pointed knife, carefully cut through the skin only from the top almost to the base.
2 Continue making cuts through the skin as above, as if marking the tomato into quarters and then eighths. These will be the 'petals'.
3 Using the top of the knife, carefully peel back the petals almost to the base. Add a tiny pile of finely chopped herbs or a few fine green chilli slices for the centre of the flower.

Tomato roses; turnip crysanthemum and cherry tomato flower

Carrot & Courgette (Zucchini) Flowers
1 Use small even-shaped vegetables. If using carrots, peel them first. Cut carrots and courgettes (zucchini) into 5cm (2 inch) lengths.
2 Using a small sharp knife, make a V-shaped cut lengthwise along the vegetable, discarding the strip that is removed. Turn the vegetable and make another lengthwise V-shaped cut, as before. Repeat a further 2 or 3 times so that there are 4 or 5 evenly spaced V-shaped grooves.
3 Thickly slice the carrots and courgettes (zucchini) to make the flower bases. Use caviar or red lumpfish roe, baby corn slices, red pepper strips or chopped radish to make the flower centres. Use chives or sprays of dill as stems.

Cut-out Flowers
1 Use fancy-shaped cutters such as diamonds, circles, petals and hearts to cut out shapes from vegetables and fruit, and vegetable skins. Red, yellow and green peppers, carrots and cucumber skins work particularly well.
2 Assemble the shapes as colourful flowers, using chives and other herbs as realistic stalks and foliage.

Courgette (zucchini) flowers; green pepper cut-out petals, red pepper cut-out flower and carrot flowers

Vegetable Purées

Smooth, fluffy vegetable purées are popular accompaniments. Particular favourites of mine are carrot or carrot with parsnip, and potato with jerusalem artichoke. As a garnish, they can be shaped into ovals or piped attractively into stars or rosettes to enhance meat and fish dishes. Alternatively, pipe into nests and fill with tiny vegetables or other savoury mixtures. Top with chopped herbs or tiny herb sprigs for maximum effect.

Duchesse Potato is a wonderful old-fashioned classic – creamy mashed potato enriched with butter and egg yolks, piped into pretty rosettes, then glazed and baked until golden and crisp on the outside but soft and light within. Use to garnish grilled or roast meat and fish, and stews.

Duchesse Potatoes & Nests

750g (1½ lb) potatoes, peeled	*pinch of freshly grated nutmeg*
60g (2oz) butter	*salt and freshly ground black*
1 egg	*pepper to taste*
2 egg yolks	*beaten egg for glazing*

1 Cut the potatoes into 4cm (1½ inch) pieces and cook in boiling salted water for about 15 minutes until soft. Drain well, then return to the pan for a few seconds to dry off.

2 Preheat the oven to 220C (425F/Gas 7). Transfer the potatoes to a mixing bowl and break up the pieces using a fork. Add the butter, egg and egg yolks and mash well or beat with an electric whisk until smooth. If necessary, press the mixture through a medium sieve to obtain a lump-free texture. Season with nutmeg, salt and pepper.

3 Using a piping bag fitted with a large fluted nozzle, pipe the mixture into rosettes or nests on a well buttered baking sheet. Bake for 10 minutes, then brush with beaten egg and bake for a further 10 minutes until golden. Serve hot. Fill potato nests as required before serving.

Potato nests, carrot purée, duchesse potato, herbed potato purée, swede purée

Vegetable Boats

Boat-shaped filled vegetables can be served hot or cold as a garnish for meat, fish, egg and vegetable dishes. Fill with a colourful vegetable mixture and tiny herb sprigs. Serve hot, basted with a little melted butter, or cold with a little vinaigrette or a dollop or mayonnaise or sour cream.

Suitable vegetables are courgettes (zucchini), broad, straight carrots and cucumber.

Courgette (Zucchini) & Carrot Boats

1 Peel carrots, if using. Halve vegetable lengthwise and cut into 7.5cm (3 inch) lengths. Using a small paring knife, chisel both ends to a point.

2 Using a teaspoon, carefully hollow out the centre of each one to give a boat shape.

3 Prepare a filling of tiny dice or julienne of vegetables – such as peppers, carrots, celery, spring onions (green shallots), peas or broccoli florets, sweetcorn, mushrooms, etc. Blanch the boats and filling vegetables until just tender if necessary; drain well. Arrange the vegetables in the boats and add herbs, if you like. Serve hot or cold.

Cucumber Boats

Use smaller, thin cucumbers. Make as above, but do not cook. Fill with dressed salad, seafood, egg, or thick, creamy dips.

Cucumber Pots

Hollowed-out pots of cucumber can be purely decorative, but they make attractive containers for dips and mayonnaise.

1 Cut a cucumber into 10cm (4 inch) lengths. Make zig-zag cuts all around the middle through the centre of the cucumber. Gently pull the halves apart.

2 From the jagged end, carefully scoop out the cucumber flesh leaving the base intact. Fill the pots with a savoury sauce or filling and/or seafood and herbs.

Cucumber boat, courgette (zucchini) boats, carrot boat and cucumber pots with savoury fillings

Potato & Poppadum Baskets

Delicate, crisp nests and baskets of golden potato are simple to make using a hinged frying basket. Fill them with sautéed or glazed vegetable and herb mixtures. Use as a garnish for hot meat, fish and poultry dishes.

Poppadum baskets are equally easy to prepare. I like to fill these with a cooling salad of cucumber, onion, tomato and herbs – to contrast spicy Indian dishes.

If you do not have a hinged frying basket (see page 4), use two small metal sieves to make the potato baskets and nests; for the poppadum nests use two long-handled spoons.

Potato Baskets

1 Peel a few medium-sized potatoes, then using a potato peeler, slice them very thinly. Soak in cold water for at least 20 minutes, then drain thoroughly and dry on a clean tea towel. Cook baskets one at a time.

2 Heat oil for deep-frying to 180C/350F. Oil a hinged frying basket and line with overlapping potato slices. Deep-fry until golden, then drain and allow to cool slightly before carefully removing the cooked potato basket. Fill before serving.

Potato Nests

Cut potato into very fine straw-like shreds; soak and drain as above. Line hinged frying basket with overlapping potato shreds. Cook and fill as above.

Poppadum Baskets

1 Use mini poppadums if possible or, with scissors, cut plain or spicy poppadums into 7.5-10cm (3-4 inch) circles.

2 Preheat oil for deep-frying to 180C/350F. Carefully hold one poppadum at a time in an oiled hinged frying basket. Deep-fry in hot oil for a few seconds so that the poppadum curls to form a golden crisp basket. Drain and cool on absorbent kitchen paper. Fill before serving.

Potato basket, poppadum basket and potato nest

Filo Containers

Baskets of paper-thin filo pastry – cooked golden and crisp – make pretty containers for savoury or sweet garnishes. Make a savoury filling of cooked vegetables or soft cheese and salad. For a sweet version fill with cream or thick yogurt and fresh or crystallized fruit. Add sprigs of herbs if you like.

Twist filo pastry squares around a cooked savoury or sweet filling to make crisp, golden purses. Use chives and other herbs to tie up baked savoury purses. Leave sweet ones plain or tie with colourful ribbon. Use as a stylish garnish.

Filo Baskets

1 Preheat oven to 190C (375F/Gas 5). Melt 60g (2oz) butter and use some to lightly grease 12 small patty tins (or bun tins). Cut 24 squares of filo pastry, each about 7.5cm (3 inches).

2 Place one square of filo pastry in each tin and brush liberally with melted butter. Give the tin a 45° turn and place a second square of filo in each tin, so it is at an angle to the first. Brush with remaining butter. Bake for 10-12 minutes until golden. Fill before serving.

Filo Purses

1 Preheat oven to 190C (375F/Gas 5). Cut 12 squares of filo pastry, each about 13cm (5 inches).

2 Brush six of the squares liberally with melted butter. Cover each one with a second square.

3 Place a spoonful of filling in the centre of each. Brush the edges of the filo with melted butter, draw up the corners to make a bundle and twist gently to secure.

4 Bake for 12-15 minutes until golden. Tie decoratively, using herbs or fine ribbon.

Filo purses; filo baskets with sweet and savoury fillings

Brandy Snap Baskets

Crisp, lacy baskets of brandy snap biscuit make attractive containers for sweet fillings. They are delicious filled with fresh fruit and cream or yogurt; ice cream and sorbet. Fill just before serving, otherwise the baskets will lose their crispness.

It is best to bake the brandy snaps four or five at a time, to avoid them hardening before you have time to shape them. Should the cooked brandy snaps become too firm to mould, soften them by reheating for a few seconds.

60g (2oz) butter
60g (2oz / ⅓ cup) light soft brown sugar
60g (2oz / 2tbsp) golden syrup

2 teaspoons brandy
2 teaspoons lemon juice
60g (2oz / ½ cup) plain flour
1 teaspoon ground ginger

1 Preheat the oven to 190C (375F/Gas 5). Put the butter, sugar, golden syrup, brandy and lemon juice into a saucepan and heat gently, stirring, until the butter melts and the sugar is dissolved. Remove from the heat and add the flour and ginger. Mix well and leave until cold.

2 Grease several baking sheets and line with non-stick paper. Have ready two or three small glasses or jars, turned upside down and lightly oiled.

3 Drop heaped teaspoonfuls of the mixture on to the baking sheets, spacing them well apart; the mixture should make about 12. Bake in the oven for 7-10 minutes until golden.

4 Allow the brandy snaps to cool slightly for a few seconds, then lift, one at a time, with a spatula and mould over an upturned glass to form a basket shape. Hold for a few seconds. Remove when firm. Fill just before serving.

Brandy snap baskets filled with fruit and sorbet

Ice

Cold and frosted, ice can be both decorative and practical too. A mountain of crushed ice piled high with freshly prepared exotic fruit makes a deliciously refreshing and simply stunning dessert. Serve shellfish in the same way for an eye-catching centrepiece. Alternatively, arrange soft and creamy goat's cheeses on crushed ice with vegetable crudités, or perhaps a little fruit.

Bowls made of ice make wonderful containers for ice creams, sorbets, fruit salads, iced soups and shellfish. Ice bowls are simple to prepare but look most impressive with fruit, flowers and herbs frozen into the ice. For a savoury version, use herbs, lemon or lime slices, shells etc.

Ice Bowl

1 Have ready two freezerproof glass bowls, one slightly smaller than the other. Select frostproof ingredients which can be frozen in the ice. Use citrus and other fruit slices, herbs, flowers and petals for a dessert container. For a shellfish bowl, choose fresh herb sprigs, mussel and clam shells, and perhaps a few whole prawns.

2 Fill the larger bowl to a depth of about 2.5cm (1 inch) with cold water. Place some decorations in the water. Position the smaller bowl inside, so it floats centrally and secure it in place with sticky tape. Freeze until solid.

3 Add more cold water to the larger bowl until it is about two-thirds full. Push more decorations into the water in between the bowls and freeze again.

4 Fill the larger bowl to the top, decorate and freeze as before.

5 To unmould the bowl, first fill the smaller bowl with luke-warm water. Twist loose and remove. To remove the outer bowl, dip it in warm water and loosen in the same way. Keep the ice bowl in the freezer until required.

Ice mountain topped with fruit salad; shellfish ice bowl; fruit and flower ice bowl

Garnishing Soups & Sauces

Soups and sauces – both savoury and sweet – are a delight to garnish. Sumptuous swirls of cream and yogurt, fresh herbs, beautiful edible flowers, tasty titbits of bacon, chopped or whole nuts, can all be casually added or formally arranged to striking and mouth-watering effect. The techniques are quite simple and are similar whether you are garnishing a tureen or bowl of soup, or an individual serving of sauce spread thinly on a plate.

For more elaborate garnishing other ingredients can be added which complement colour, flavour and texture. For savoury soups and sauces, arrange attractive borders using herb sprigs, clusters of tiny vegetable dice or julienne. Delicate piles of caviar, especially salmon caviar, look attractive on fish dishes. Try an arrangement of alternate piles of red and black lumpfish roe for a very colourful border effect.

Cream Swirls & Shapes

Guests always think there is some secret talent required to float a swirl of cream or yogurt on top of a soup or sauce but this is not the case. The only secret is to have the cream thick enough to hold its shape. Use double (thick) cream, giving it a good stir so that it thickens a little but will still pour from the spoon. If using yogurt, choose the thick Greek variety. Simply start at the centre of the soup or sauce and swirl outwards, in a spiral if you like.

To achieve a 'feathery' effect have a cocktail stick at the ready. Make a swirl then lightly draw the cocktail stick through the edges to give a wispy look.

To create petals or heart shapes of cream or yogurt, carefully float round dollops on the soup or sauce and draw a cocktail stick or skewer in one vertical stroke through each dollop.

Soup garnishes: cream swirl with snipped chives and rosemary; cream petal with tied chives; feathered cream swirl

Spider's Web
A spider's web pattern of cream is particularly striking and still quite simple to achieve. It is most effective as a decoration for sweet sauces on individual dessert plates.

As well as with cream and yogurt products, this effect can also be achieved using two sauces in contrasting colours, but any type of feathering will only work well on velvet smooth sauces and purées.

1 Pour sauce on to a serving plate and swivel the plate to spread the sauce evenly over the base. Place lightly whipped cream in a small greaseproof paper piping bag and snip off the tip.

2 Pipe three or four concentric circles of cream on to the plate of sauce. Draw a skewer through the cream from the centre to the plate edge, or from one side of the plate to the other at regular intervals, wiping the skewer clean after each use.

Other ideas for Sweet Sauces
Arrange tiny piles of julienne or diced fruit or peel around the edge of the plate. Whole small pretty fruits such as raspberries, fraise de bois, pomegranate seeds, blueberries and summer currants will cheer even the simplest custard. Alternatively use frosted flowers and petals, glacé fruits, chocolate curls and leaves.

Sweet sauces can be decorative in themselves – try serving contrasting fruit sauces, as shown opposite, or combine dark and white chocolate sauces in the same way.

Garnishes for sweet sauces: chocolate sauce with heart-shaped cream dollops; contrasting fruit sauces with cluster of summer fruits; cream spider's web enhancing fruit sauce

Croûtons

A favourite London restaurant serves its Coq au Vin garnished with a large croûton in the shape of a cockerel. I am always delighted by this personal, off-beat touch.

Crunchy golden croûtons are superb tossed into salads and sprinkled over soups; they also make good garnishes for egg dishes. Use larger croûtons as bases for grilled meat and small game birds, or canapés. Cut out shaped croûtons if you like and serve plain, or flavoured with garlic, herbs, paprika, Parmesan cheese or other seasonings.

Plain Croûtons
1 Cut day-old white or wholemeal bread into cubes, or shapes using small cutters.
2 Heat a few tablespoons of olive oil and a large knob of butter in a small frying pan. To test the temperature, drop in one piece of bread – it should sizzle gently as soon as you add it. Add the bread and stir constantly until the croûtons are an even golden brown colour. Drain on absorbent kitchen paper.

Garlic Croûtons
Add 1 – 2 crushed garlic cloves to the pan before cooking.

Herbed Croûtons
Cook and drain as above. Dip half of each croûton into very finely chopped parsley or other herbs, or simply sprinkle herbs over cubed croûtons.

Flavoured Croûtons
Cook as for plain croûtons and while hot, drop straight from the pan into a paper bag containing salt and chopped herbs or other seasonings. Shake until the croûtons are coated. Seasonings to try are paprika, freshly grated Parmesan cheese, celery salt, toasted sesame seeds and poppy seeds.

Plain and shaped, herbed and Parmesan flavoured croûtons

Pastry Garnishes

Pastry garnishes, glazed and golden baked to perfection, always look good whether used to decorate a pie, or as a pastry 'fleuron' to accompany casseroles and other meat, or fish dishes cooked in sauce.

Pastry Shapes
Use cutters or a knife to cut out pastry shapes; mould berries, for example, with your hands. Simply mark on patterns with a knife. Choose decorations to reflect the nature of the dish: fish shapes for fish pies; holly leaves and berries for festive pies; tiny moulded fruit shapes for fruit pies, etc.

Decorative Borders
Attractive borders for pies and flans can also be made using pastry leftovers. Twist two equal lengths of pastry to form a 'rope' or work three lengths together in a 'plait'. Criss-cross equal-sized strips to create a decorative lattice pattern.

Pastry Tassels
These are easy to make and look fun baked onto pies and tarts. Cut a pastry strip about 15cm (6 inches) long and 5cm (2 inches) wide. Cut slits along one side to look like 'fringing' and then roll up the strip, place it on the pie and open out the tassels.

Pastry Fleurons
1 Preheat the oven to 220C (425F/Gas 7). Roll out puff pastry and cut out shapes such as crescents, hearts and fluted rounds, using pastry cutters. Cut out squares and triangles using a sharp knife.
2 Use the back of a knife blade to mark a criss-cross pattern on each pastry shape. Place well apart on a baking sheet and brush with beaten egg to glaze. Bake for 8-10 minutes or until well risen and golden brown.

Cut-out and moulded pastry shapes; pastry fleurons; pastry tassels

Fresh Fruit Garnishes

Just one sumptuous strawberry can transform an individual dessert. So too can summer berries, delicate currants on the stem, cherries and clusters of grapes. To simply slice other fruits, such as kiwi, star fruit, peaches, citrus fruits, pawpaw and kumquats, is enough to make a pretty garnish.

Use fruits to decorate sweet and savoury dishes – especially citrus fruits, apricots, peaches, raspberries and currants. On party platters anything goes, visual appeal is all.

Choose fruits that are just ripe, but still firm and blemish-free. For maximum effect use the fruit leaves too if you can. Otherwise replace with mint or other greenery, such as lemon balm, sweet cicely, or geranium.

Fruit Fans

Use to decorate gâteaux, mousses, soufflés, cheesecakes, ices, sorbets and other desserts, as well as salads, buffet platters and meat or fish dishes with fruit sauces.

Suitable fruits are strawberries, peaches, nectarines, kiwi fruit, mango, paw-paw and poached pears.

Strawberry Fans
Using a small sharp knife and keeping the stalk end intact, cut five or six lengthwise slices. Gently flatten the strawberry to fan out. If the strawberry stalk is less than perfect replace it with a mint sprig.

Peach or Nectarine Fans
1 Cut the fruit around the middle, then twist gently to separate the halves. Discard the stone. Cut each half in two to give quarter wedges.
2 Keeping one end of each wedge intact, cut five or six lengthwise slices. Flatten gently to fan out and finish with a herb sprig.

Strawberry fans, nectarine fans and kiwi fan (page 58)

56

Kiwi Fans
Peel a kiwi fruit and quarter lengthwise. Holding one end of each wedge intact, cut five or six lengthwise slices. Flatten gently to fan out. (Illustrated on page 57).

Mango Fans
1 Peel a mango and cut in half either side of the large stone. At a slight angle, cut each half crosswise into three pieces.
2 Keeping one end of each mango piece intact, cut four or five lengthwise slices. Flatten gently to fan out. Finish with a raspberry, a strawberry slice, a cluster of redcurrants or a herb sprig.

Paw-Paw Fans
1 Peel and halve the fruit lengthwise. Using a teaspoon carefully scoop out the black seeds. Place the halves cut side down on the serving plate and cut each half crosswise into three pieces.
2 Cut four or five slices across the width of each piece, keeping one end intact. Press gently to flatten and fan out the slices.

Fanned Poached Pears
Slightly sweet poached pears make an attractive garnish for roast pork, poultry and game birds and cured delicatessen meats. Choose firm but ripe pears.
1 Peel and halve the fruit. Scoop out the core from each half using a melon baller or teaspoon. Coat with lemon juice to prevent discolouring.
2 Poach the pears in a light sugar syrup, or red or rosé wine which has been sweetened with a little honey, for 10-15 minutes until tender. Drain well.
3 Leaving the stalk end intact, cut each pear half lengthwise into five slices. Flatten gently to fan out.

Fanned poached pear, paw-paw fans and mango fan

Fruit Flowers

Fruit flowers make splendid decorations for gâteaux, cheese-cakes, flans, ice creams, sorbets and a host of other desserts. They are also ideal garnishes for savoury buffet platters.
Suitable fruit are figs, starfruit and kiwi fruit.

Starfruit Flowers
1 Simply slice a starfruit (carambola) and a few kumquats. Place a kumquat slice on each 'star'.
2 Use chives or strips of cucumber peel to make stalks, and mint or other herbs as leaves if you like.

Fig Flowers
Green or purple ripe figs with dark red centres opened to resemble flowers make a wonderful garnish for summer fruit desserts, cheese boards and parma ham.

1 Stand a fig upright and using a small sharp knife, cut vertically into four wedges, leaving the base intact. Open out the wedges to form petals.
2 Add a dollop of thick yogurt or cream to the centre of the flower, or finish with a sprig of mint or other herb.

Kiwi Fruit Lillies
Choose a firm kiwi fruit. Using a small pointed knife, make connecting V-shaped cuts all around the middle of the fruit, cutting right through to the centre. Gently pull the two halves apart.

Starfruit flowers, fig flowers and kiwi fruit lily

Citrus Fruit Garnishes

Lemons, limes, grapefruit, oranges, tangerines, clementines and kumquats: citrus fruits lend themselves wonderfully to garnishing. They are mostly available all year round and their colours add instant freshness to sweet and savoury foods and drinks alike. A simple wedge of lemon or lime is the perfect garnish for dishes which require a squeeze of fresh juice such as fresh fish and shellfish, smoked fish, oriental foods, salads, crêpes, and the very sweet exotic fruits such as prickly pear, sharon fruit and paw-paw. A multitude of citrus garnishes, such as twists, segments and butterflies, are also very simple to prepare.

Using a Canelle Knife
A canelle knife is a special tool for removing 'grooves' from citrus peel. These give a pretty scalloped effect to citrus fruit slices, an attractive striped look to whole fruit or wedges, and the strips of peel that are removed can be coiled into spirals for garnishing too. Simply remove the strips of peel before cutting the fruit.

Citrus Twists
Cut the fruit into slices about 5mm (¼ inch) thick. With a sharp knife, make a cut in each slice almost to the centre. Twist each side of the cut in opposite directions.

If you like, group together two or three citrus slices before 'twisting'.

Citrus Cones
Use oranges, tangerines, clementines, lemons and limes. Prepare and cut slices as for citrus twists (above). Overlap cut edges to form a cone shape. Secure with a cocktail stick. Place a tiny herb sprig or a few fine shreds of contrasting citrus peel inside each cone, if you like.

Lemon and lime twists; lemon and lime cones

Citrus Bows

Use oranges, tangerines, clementines, lemons and limes.

1 Slice the fruit and then cut each slice in half. Make another cut in each half slice as if to quarter, but do not quite cut through the centre, to give two joined triangles.

2 Position the triangles to look like a bow-tie.

3 To finish the 'bows', place a tiny knot of chive or pimento in the centre of each one, or position 2.5cm (1 inch) lengths of chive as shown.

Orange & Grapefruit Segments

1 Using a sharp knife remove a thin slice from the top and base of the fruit, cutting to reveal the flesh. Stand the fruit on its base.

2 Remove the skin and white pith by cutting off the skin in slices in a downward motion.

3 Remove the segments by cutting into the fruit close to each side of the membranes of the segments. Use the knife to ease out each segment.

Citrus Julienne

Fine julienne of citrus peel look fresh and elegant as a garnish for meat, fish and poultry dishes, oriental foods and vegetables, ice creams, sorbets, cakes, mousses and other desserts. You can scatter them over soups and salads too.

1 Using a sharp knife cut the peel thinly from the fruit. Scrape away as much of the white pith as possible from the peel.

2 Trim the peel into even-sized rectangles and then cut into fine julienne threads.

3 Blanch in boiling water for 1 minute then refresh in cold water and dry thoroughly on absorbent kitchen paper.

Orange segments; lemon and lime bows

Fruits as Containers

Fruit dishes served in their natural containers always look impressive. Citrus fruit shells lend themselves particularly well. Remove a slice from the top and hollow out the whole fruit, or half lemons lengthwise for a more elegant boat-like container. Clementines, tangerines, small oranges and limes make pretty containers too. Fill them with creamy light mousses or tiny balls of ice cream or sorbet, scooped using a melon baller.

Thirst-quenching melon sorbet can be eaten like fresh melon wedges. Simply halve the fruit and scoop out the flesh. Pack the prepared sorbet into the shell halves and freeze.

Apricot, peach and nectarine halves piled with soft berry fruits make a delightful summer garnish that is simple to prepare. Try serving exotic fruit salad in paw-paw shells too.

Lemon or Lime Baskets
Tiny baskets carved from lemons or limes make an unusual, eye-catching garnish for sweet or savoury dishes. For seafood and oriental dishes fill the baskets with herbs and/or salad vegetables, and perhaps a whole cooked prawn or pretty clam. For sweet dishes fill with small prepared fruits and mint sprigs or frosted flowers and leaves. Edible flowers look effective in these delicate baskets too.

1 Select a blemish-free lemon or lime. Holding the fruit on its side make a vertical cut slightly off centre half way through the fruit. Make a horizontal cut to meet the base of the first cut. Remove the wedge of fruit.

2 Repeat on the other side, to create a basket shape.

3 Carefully scoop out all the fruit flesh to reveal a basket with handle. Fill the basket as required.

Lemon basket filled with cucumber, peach slices, rosemary and chilli flower; apricot half topped with peach slices, raspberries and mint; lime basket filled with berry fruits and frosted flowers and leaves

Chocolate Decorations

When it comes to decorating gâteaux and desserts, piling on the chocolate is sure to bring gasps of delight. My favourite chocolate decoration is really a cheat: delicious alcoholic truffles – dusted with cocoa and icing sugar – transform any dessert into something special!

Making your own chocolate decorations – curls, caraque, leaves, shapes and piped doodles – is fun. Best results come from using a good quality dark patissière chocolate, but you can use milk or white chocolate if you prefer.

Always handle chocolate with care. Melt it very gently away from direct heat using a heatproof bowl over a pan of simmering water. Chocolate can easily be melted in the microwave on a low setting too. Be sure to keep decorations in a cool place, but not the refrigerator.

Simple Chocolate Curls
Use a chunky-sized bar of good quality chocolate at room temperature. With a potato peeler, scrape small curls from the side of the chocolate bar on to a chilled plate.

Chocolate Caraque
1 Pour melted chocolate onto a marble slab or other cold smooth surface.
2 Using a palette knife spread the chocolate thinly into a rectangular shape. Leave to cool until matt and firm, but not hard or brittle.
3 Hold a sharp long-bladed knife at both ends and draw it across the chocolate towards you with the knife tilted backwards at a slight angle to shave off long, thin scrolls.

Chocolate Rose Leaves
1 Rinse and dry rose leaves. Using a small dry brush, coat the underside of each leaf with melted chocolate.
2 Leave to set, coated side uppermost. When hard, carefully peel away the leaves.

Assorted chocolate rose leaves, curls and caraque

Chocolate Shapes

1 Cover a chopping board or marble slab with non-stick paper or foil, keeping the surface as smooth as possible.

2 Pour melted chocolate on to the paper or foil and tilt the board to spread it smoothly and evenly. Leave until set, but not brittle.

3 Cut out squares and triangles using a ruler and a sharp knife. Use metal cutters to cut out circles, hearts and other shapes.

Piped Chocolate Designs

Melted chocolate can be piped into delicate shapes and used for decorating desserts, cakes and petits fours. Doodle dainty hearts and flowers or try simple butterflies and birds. You can also write names and messages but you'll need a bit of a steady hand!

1 Place melted chocolate in a greaseproof piping bag. Snip off a tiny point from the tip to give a fine writing 'nozzle'.

2 Pipe simple shapes or letters directly onto non-stick paper. For more elaborate chocolate shapes, first write or draw the design in pencil on the paper as many times as required. Pipe the chocolate over the marked designs.

3 Leave until set hard, then carefully peel away the paper or lift the shapes with a palette knife.

Piped chocolate butterfly, abstract design and heart; cut-out chocolate triangles, square, circles and heart

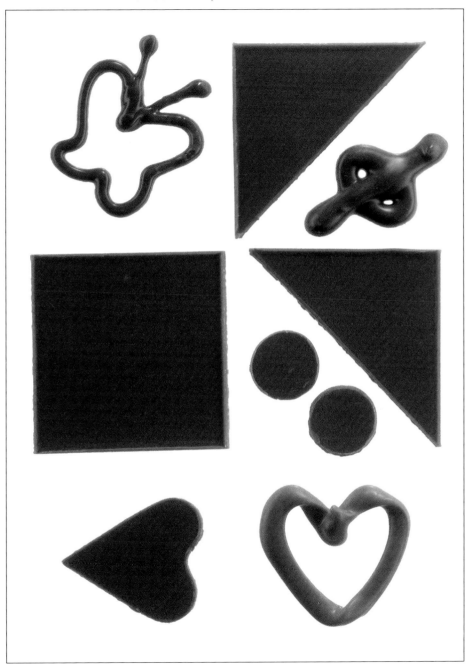

Nuts & Praline

Nuts are such a versatile garnishing ingredient. They can be scattered, whole or chopped, over salads, soups and vegetable dishes. Toasted pine nuts glisten like amber jewels in a dressed crisp salad. Flakes of almond are delicious scattered over fish, curries and other ethnic dishes. Nuts marry well with cheeses. Try sandwiching soft cheese between walnut or pecan halves, or roll cheese balls in chopped nuts.

All kinds of nuts can be used to decorate cakes, ices and other desserts, whether you choose peanuts or pistachios, almonds, walnuts, hazelnuts, pecans, brazils or macadamias. Use them grated, toasted, halved or chopped. Grated pistachio with its delicate green colour looks wonderful sprinkled over frothy cocktails, desserts and petits fours.

Nuts are the perfect partner for chocolate. Pecans, walnuts, toasted hazelnuts, macadamias and brazils work well; browned or 'burnt' almonds are also superb with chocolate. Try chocolate coated and caramelized nuts too.

Praline

Praline can be broken into jagged pieces or ground to a coarse powder and used to decorate all kinds of sweet dishes. Choose from pecans, roasted almonds, hazelnuts, walnuts or pistachios, or use a combination.

1 Preheat oven to 180C (350F/Gas 4). Lightly oil a baking sheet and set aside. Spread 250g (8oz) nuts on a clean baking sheet and warm in the oven for 5 minutes.

2 Meanwhile, put 250g (8oz) granulated sugar in a heavy-based saucepan with 75ml (2½fl oz / ⅓ cup) water. Place over a low heat until the sugar has dissolved, then bring to the boil and cook, without stirring, for 6-8 minutes until the syrup turns a rich golden colour. Remove from the heat.

3 Add the nuts to the pan and stir to coat in the caramel. Pour on to the oiled baking sheet and leave to set. Break into pieces or grind to a coarse powder.

Mixed nut praline, almond praline and pecan cheese balls

Chocolate-dipped & Caramelized Fruit & Nuts

Fresh fruits and nuts which have been coated with dark, milk or white chocolate, or with a dark golden crisp caramel make splendid decorations for gâteaux, cheesecakes, mousses and other elaborate desserts.

Fruits and nuts suitable for dipping are strawberries, cherries, grapes, tangerine or clementine segments, Cape gooseberry, kumquats, brazil nuts, walnuts and toasted almonds.

Ensure the fruit is clean and dry. If grapes are small leave in clusters of two or three, if you like. Leave stalks on cherries and strawberries. To prepare Cape gooseberry use small scissors to snip the papery skin into 'petals', peel back to reveal the fruit and secure with a twist.

Chocolate-dipped Fruit & Nuts

Melt plain (dark), milk or white chocolate in a bowl over hot water. Spear fruit or nuts on to bamboo skewers and partially dip into the melted chocolate to half-coat. Leave to set on non-stick paper. Use within 8 hours.

Caramelized Fruit & Nuts

1 Put 375g (12oz/1½ cups) granulated sugar and 90ml (3floz/⅓ cup) water in a heavy-based pan over a low heat until the sugar is dissolved.

2 Bring to the boil and cook, without stirring, for about 7-8 minutes until golden in colour; do not allow the caramel to become too dark. Stand the saucepan in a bowl of warm water to prevent the caramel hardening.

3 Spear the fruit or nuts on to bamboo skewers and dip into the caramel to coat completely. Leave to set on non-stick paper. Use within 6 hours.

Chocolate-dipped pecans, tangerine segments, strawberry and Cape gooseberry; caramelized grapes, Brazil nuts, walnut and strawberry

Frosted Fruits & Flowers

Fresh fruit and small blossoms glistening with a coat of fine sugar make desserts look irresistible. Frosting fruits and flowers is a simple affair and the results are subtly stunning. Shop-bought decorations can never compare. The easiest method of frosting uses only egg white and caster sugar. Fruits and flowers prepared in this way should be used the same day as they are made. For flowers that will store in airtight containers for several months follow instructions for crystallised flowers (page 78).

Frosted Fruits

Fruits suitable for frosting are clusters of grapes, currants on the stem, strawberries, clementine segments, gooseberries, Cape gooseberries and cherries. If using Cape gooseberry, peel back the papery skin to reveal the fruit and secure with a twist. Wash fruit and dry thoroughly.

1 Lightly beat an egg white until just frothy. Use a soft paintbrush to coat the fruit with the egg white.

2 Stand the fruit on a plate or non-stick paper dusted with caster sugar. Thickly dredge with more sugar and gently shake off the excess. Place the fruit on a wire rack covered with greaseproof paper and leave to dry.

Frosted Flowers

Whole flowers or individual petals can be frosted. Suitable flowers are roses, sweet peas, freesias, primrose, violets, borage flowers, polyanthus and geraniums. Leaves and herbs such as mint, lemon balm and scented geranium leaves are also suitable.

Make sure flowers and leaves are fresh and dry. Trim stems and separate the flower petals if you wish to frost them individually. Prepare as for frosting fruits (above).

Frosted grapes, leaf, rosebud, roses, Cape gooseberry, strawberry and clementine segment

Crystallized Fruits

These are well worth a mention but unless you love to eat them as a candy, I do not recommend making them at home because the preparation is a lengthy procedure. All manner of crystallized fruits – from pineapples to kiwis to greengages – can be bought from good pâtisseries and delicatessens. Expensive, yes, but for decorating gâteaux and desserts a little goes a long way.

Angelica is a popular decoration for desserts and cakes. Stem ginger, preserved in syrup is another favourite. Slice it thinly, shred or dice to decorate ice creams, desserts or gâteaux, and trickle a little of the syrup over if you like.

Crystallized Flowers

These are identical in appearance to frosted flowers (illustrated on previous page) but crystallized flowers have the advantage that they can be stored for up to 3 months.

The following quantity of coating is sufficient for the petals of 3-4 roses or equivalent. You will need about 500g (1lb) caster sugar.

1 Dissolve 2 teaspoons gum arabic in 4 teaspoons rose water or orange flower water.

2 Use a soft paintbrush to coat the petals of flowers, two or three at a time, with the solution.

3 Stand the flowers on a plate or non-stick paper dusted with caster sugar and thickly dredge with more sugar. Gently shake off the excess.

4 Leave the flowers on a fine-meshed rack, or wire rack lined with greaseproof paper, in a warm place to dry and become brittle.

5 Store on tissue paper in an airtight tin, for up to 3 months.

Crystallized pineapple, pear, clementine wedges, orange slice, cherries, lemon slice, stem ginger and angelica

Index

Avocado fans 26
Basil 6
Bâtons, vegetable 24
Boats, vegetable 38
Borage 6
Brandy snap baskets 44
Bundles, vegetable 20

Canelle knife 4; to use 62
Caramelized fruit and nuts 74
Carrot and courgette flowers 34
Celery tassels 28
Cherry tomato flower 32
Chervil 6
Chilli flower 30
Chinese garlic chives 8
Chiselled vegetables 24
Chives 8
Chocolate decorations 68-70
Chocolate-dipped fruit and nuts 74
Citrus fruit garnishes 62, 64
Citrus julienne 64
Coriander 8
Courgette and carrot boats 38
Cream swirls and shapes 48
Croûtons 52
Cystallized fruits and flowers 78
Cucumber boats or pots 38
Cucumber fans or fleurs-de-lys 26
Cucumber twists 26
Curls, vegetable 22
Cut-out flowers 34

Dill 10
Duchesse potatoes and nests 36

Fans, fruit 56, 58; vegetable 26
Fennel 10
Fig flowers 60
Filo containers 42
Flowers, crystallized 78;
    cut from fruit 60;
    from vegetables 30, 34
Frosted fruits and flowers 76

Garlic chives 8
Gherkin fans 26

Ice bowl 46

Julienne bundles 20
Julienne vegetables 18

Kiwi fans 58
Kiwi fruit lillies 60

Lemon balm 10
Lemon or lime baskets 66

Mango fans 58
Marigold 10
Marjoram 12
Mint 12

Nasturtium 12
Nuts 72

Oregano 12

Parsley 14
Pastry garnishes 54
Paw-paw fans 58
Peach or nectarine fans 56
Pears, fanned poached 58
Poppadum baskets 40
Potato:
    Chiselled potatoes 24
    Duchesse potatoes and nests 36
    Pommes allumettes 18
    Potato baskets and nests 40
Praline 72
Purées, vegetable 36

Radish bud or flower 30
Ribbons, vegetable 22
Rosemary 14

Sage 14
Scented geranium 16
Soup and sauce garnishes 48, 50
Spirals, vegetable 22
Spring onion tassels 28
Starfruit flowers 60
Strawberry fans 56
Sweet, cicely 16

Tarragon 16
Tassels, pastry 54;
    vegetable 28
Thyme 16
Tomato rose 32
Turnip chrysanthemum 32